Dreaming Place

Story by Dawn McMillan

Illustrations by Virginia Gray

Rigby PM Plus Chapter Books
part of the Rigby PM Program
Sapphire Level

Published by Rigby
a division of Harcourt Supplemental Publishers, Inc.
1000 Hart Road
Barrington, IL 60010-2627
www.rigby.com

U.S. edition © 2004 Rigby
a division of Harcourt Supplemental Publishers, Inc.

First published in 2003 by Thomson Learning Australia
Text © Nelson Australia Pty Ltd 2003
Illustrations © Thomson Learning Australia 2003

10 9 8 7 6 5 4 3 2 1
07 06 05 04 03

Printed in China by Midas Printing (Asia) Ltd

The Dreaming Place
ISBN 0 75786 929 7

Contents

Chapter One
Leah's Story

My name is Leah. My friends say I should tell my story because it might help other people. Amy is really anxious for me to do it, and so is Kayla.

"It might get published in a book!" Kayla says.

I'm nervous about sharing my feelings and experiences. I'm not sure that I can write well enough to tell the story. Amy and Kayla say, "You'll never know unless you try!" and "Come on, Leah! You know about taking a risk!"

So here I am, at the computer. I'm not much of a typist, as I only use three fingers, but I can go quite fast. I can only have the computer for an hour each night, because in our big family, we have to take turns.

Our English teacher says the first part of a story is the hardest part to write. I agree with her! I've used up half of my time just thinking about a title. I think I'll settle for *The Dreaming Place*, as that's where my story begins.

I was nine when I found my special dreaming place. It was out in the orchard — my own private gymnasium! Around the old trees the grass grew strong and thick, making a spongy tumbling mat under my feet. The long, low branches of the apple tree were my horizontal bars, and the old logs lying on the ground were the beams where I practiced my balances and turns.

Most afternoons after school, I went to my dreaming place. I had seen the gymnasts on television competing in the Olympic Games, and I had dreams of being just like them. As I somersaulted and cartwheeled in the grass, I saw myself at the Games, tumbling across the mat in time with the music. I imagined the noise of the crowd as the judges called my scores:

9.8   9.8   9.8   9.7   9.9

In my dream, I stood proudly on the presentation platform, with a medal around my neck and flowers in my hands.

Sometimes I asked my older sisters, Sarah and Elizabeth, to come to my dreaming place. We did gymnastics together, but I never told them about my dreams.

I knew I needed lessons if I was to become a skilled gymnast, so I asked Mom and Dad if I could join the gymnastics club in town.

"Soon, Leah," Dad said. "We just need to get the car paid for, then you can have your lessons."

But something happened, and my dreams were shattered!

Chapter Two
The Accident

I don't remember the accident. It's so strange because I can remember that day at school very clearly. We had our swim meet and our team won! It was our under-ten meet, and when it was my turn, I swam really fast. I could hear the crowd yelling and cheering!

I wanted to get home quickly to share the news with Mom and Dad. I remember taking my bike from the rack, putting on my helmet, and setting off down the road.

The first thing I remember after that is waking up in a strange place, and feeling as if I'd been away for a long time. As I opened my eyes, the walls came up close, then went back again. I could hear Mom and Dad calling me.

"Leah! Leah!" Their voices went back and forth, too — just like the walls.

"Where am I?" I asked, sounding scratchy and loud.

"You're in the hospital, Leah," Dad whispered.

I tried to sit up, but a nurse put her hand gently on my shoulder.

I must have slipped back into sleep, because the next thing I knew, the room was dark. Someone was sitting in the chair beside the bed. I turned my face and saw Dad in the shadows. His head was slumped forward and he was snoring gently.

"Dad!" I called, and he sat bolt upright.

"You're awake!" he exclaimed. "Leah! I'm so glad you're all right!"

"Where's Mom?" I asked. "I want Mom, too!" I cried. I lifted my hand to wipe my eyes and I felt the tube clipped to my arm. Suddenly I was afraid.

"What happened to me, Dad?" I screamed. There was a pain in my side and I reached over toward my shoulder.

Dad snatched my hand and held it tightly in his hand. "Mom went home for a shower," he said. "She'll be back soon, I promise!"

I remember a nurse giving me an injection, and then I drifted into that sleepy feeling again. Somewhere in the background I heard Mom arrive.

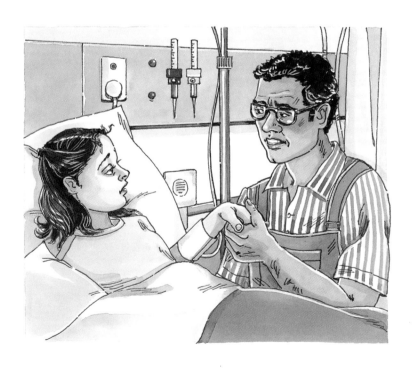

Chapter Three
Facing the Truth

All this was three years ago, but I still remember the pain as they told me what had happened. The words floated past me on a dark, foggy cloud.

In the morning light, I could see that on one side of my bed the cover was high over a pillow. On the other side, my arm was on top of the bedclothes. Mom was holding my hand.

"What happened?" I asked, already afraid to know the truth.

"You had a very bad accident, Leah," Dad began. "You turned across the road and a truck hit you."

Mom's face was ashen. "You've lost your arm, darling," she whispered.

My arm! What did they mean, I'd lost my arm? I reached over and lifted the blanket. Alongside the pillow I saw a space where my arm should have been, a clean white area of sheet. I looked again, wanting to see my elbow, my hand! And then I screamed!

At the hospital, I had lots of visitors. Kayla and Amy brought me flowers and my favorite chocolate bars.

"Can't wait to have you back at school!" Amy said.

Kayla was very quiet. I wanted to say, "Why are you so miserable? It's not your arm that's gone!" But I didn't.

The other kids from school came, too, and the teachers, but none of them mentioned my arm. Everyone said something like, "Hope you're feeling better."

But I wasn't feeling better! And I didn't want to go to school, not ever!

It was hard for Mom and Dad, Elizabeth and Sarah, and for my brothers, David and Wills. They didn't say much, but at least they didn't tell me how I should feel. They just sat with me and loved me.

Nana was the one I talked to. I told her how angry I was. I told her that the doctors should have been able to fix my arm, and that my life was ruined!

"The doctors worked so hard, Leah," Nana said. "There was nothing more they could do. Your arm was too badly damaged."

Going home was like starting life again. In my room, I sat on the bed to take my shoes off. Then I realized that if I untied the laces, I wouldn't be able to tie them up again! If I couldn't tie laces, what else wouldn't I be able to do? How would I write, cut up my food, peel my orange, tie up my hair? The list went on in my mind, and I felt panic sweep over me.

"We'll get the help that you need, Leah," Mom said. "You'll find new ways of doing things."

I didn't want help. I just wanted it all to go away! I ran out to my dreaming place, sat on the soft grass, and cried my dreams away. I would never be a gymnast now.

Chapter Four
On the Outside

Amy and Kayla looked after me when I first went back to school. We walked around together, but they kept watching the lunchtime games.

One day I said to them, "Go on. I know you want to play." They both looked embarrassed.

"But what about you, Leah?" Amy asked.

I felt my face going red. "Don't you feel sorry for me!" I shouted at her.

Poor Amy. I look back now and wonder why she stayed my friend, but I'm glad she did.

All that year, I felt like I was on the outside of everything. The school provided me with my own computer, but even that made me feel different. I refereed the hockey games and the basketball games, but it wasn't the same as playing. In the pool, I learned to enjoy the water again, but no one asked me to swim in a race. At the swim meets, I announced the events. I know I was given the job to make me feel important, and that people were trying to make me feel better.

Some days I did feel happier, but then the dark moods would come back. I felt so angry with myself for making such a terrible mistake on the way home from school. I wanted to turn the clock back and be whole again.

Mom and Dad thought counseling might help me, and it did a bit. It was good to have someone who really listened to how I felt. I didn't want to talk about it with Mom and Dad. They had enough worries already. The counselor and Nana were the only people I shared my real feelings with.

But there was one thing that I couldn't share with anyone, and that was the dream I had practiced in the orchard.

Chapter Five
Starting Again

On summer vacation, I started going to my dreaming place again. The sweet scent of the summer grasses brought the old dreams back and I tried some somersaults. I practiced and practiced, learning to roll evenly along my spine, and I became less nervous about hurting the stump of my arm. I practiced the beam work, too. Then I heard the music again and made up a dance.

"You're smiling again, Leah," Mom laughed, and Sarah and Elizabeth hugged me as if they knew my secret.

When school started again, Miss Skelton was there. "You must be Leah," she said quietly.

"You know me because I'm the only one here with one arm!" I snapped.

"That's right," was all she said.

I liked Miss Skelton right away. I felt as if I could trust her, that she wouldn't say things just to try and make me feel better.

"So how is it for you, Leah?" she asked.

"I can't do much!" I replied, trying not to cry.

"What about a prosthesis arm?" Miss Skelton asked gently.

"I tried some, but my stump's too small, and I didn't like them strapped across my back!" I explained.

Miss Skelton nodded. Then I told her about feeling different from the other kids.

"Different?" she asked.

"Like I'm not good enough anymore!" I muttered.

"Of course you're good enough, Leah," Miss Skelton reassured me. "Have you ever thought that the others might not feel good enough to take care of you?"

I stared at Miss Skelton. I hadn't thought of it like that before, and I felt ashamed about all the times that I had been so rude.

"I think you need to learn some new skills," Miss Skelton said gently.

All that fall, Miss Skelton and I worked together to develop my new skills. I learned to swim straight by changing my body position for balance. I never made the relay team, but I did enter the freestyle, and I finished the race without crashing into anyone!

As the weather grew colder and winter sports started, I learned to catch a ball to my chest, to turn it in my left hand, and pass it out again. It took a long time before I could get my passes long and straight, as my left hand felt clumsy. Sometimes I wanted to use my right hand and I forgot it wasn't there.

Then I wanted to yell, "I'm not doing this anymore!" But I didn't!

I learned how to hold a hockey stick with my one hand placed lower down the stick for more control. There were times when I lost my balance and seemed to get my feet mixed up. I couldn't understand how working with just one arm could mix my feet up! But I practiced and practiced, and Amy, Kayla, and my other friends helped me.

I played in some real field hockey and basketball games that winter. It was so exciting! I forgot about having only one arm, and I think the others did, too.

Chapter Six
Catching Dreams

The year flew by, and when the next summer came, I asked Sarah and Elizabeth to join me in the orchard. Sarah looked at me in surprise when I showed her my beam work.

"I never knew you could do that, Leah!" she exclaimed. "Why don't you show Mom and Dad?"

"You should take those gymnastic lessons you wanted!" Elizabeth said excitedly.

I changed the subject quickly. "Watch me tumble!" I said, and over and over I went.

I wonder if Elizabeth told Miss Skelton about my gymnastics, because not long after that gymnastics classes started at school. I sat against the wall of the gymnasium, and held my dreams to my chest. I could take risks with basketball and field hockey, but I couldn't risk failing at gym.

After class one day, Miss Skelton took me aside. "I have a feeling that you're keeping something from us, Leah. On Friday I'm going to be looking for the five best gymnasts in our school. I need to make up a team to perform for the end-of-year show. We'll be having the auditions for the floor exercises at lunchtime." With that, she turned and walked out of the gymnasium.

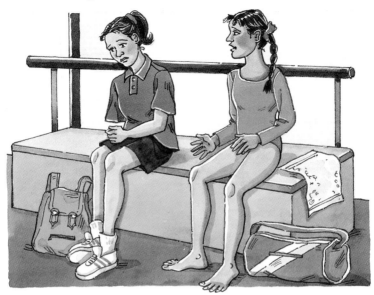

On Friday, everyone was excited about the auditions. I went to watch, and Kayla was fantastic! She looked wonderful in her blue leotard as she jumped and tumbled. She sat down beside me and puffed, "I wish you could do it, Leah! It's magic!"

We watched together as the others each had their turn, and then it was over.

Suddenly I knew what I had to do. I stood up and walked over to Miss Skelton.

"Can you put the music on again, please?" I asked, and walked to the edge of the mat.

The first bars of music sounded like the wind on a summer's day. Suddenly I was back in the orchard, in my dreaming place. I leaped and tumbled across the floor, walked an imaginary beam in perfect balance, and tossed my head as I sank to the mat for the final chord.

Then the cheering began. I felt like a winner, my school shorts and shirt transformed into a purple leotard, and my gold medal, the light from Miss Skelton's face.

"My goodness, Leah! You are a surprise!" she laughed.

It's a year later and I'm still on the gymnastics team. We do demonstrations for community events, and I think we're a little bit famous! I love the floor exercises, but I've got a new dream now. I've discovered the ribbon event. I like the way the colors flow together, and I can twist my wrist to change the patterns. One day I might take my ribbons to the Paralympics!

So this is my story. It's a story about getting a dream back — but most of all, it's a story about love and people taking care of each other.